CLASSIC CARS

CELEBRATING THE LEGENDS

Tim Slade

igloo

igloo

Published in 2010
by Igloo Books Ltd
Cottage Farm,
Sywell,
NN6 0JB.
www.igloo-books.com

© Igloo Books Ltd 2006

ISBN 978-1-84852-957-1

10 9 8 7 6 5 4 3 2 1

Project management by: Metro Media Ltd
Editorial and design management: Cecilia Thom
Author: Tim Slade
Sub-Editors: Cyrus Shahrad, Cecilia Thom
Layout: Richard Reid, Z Swaleh, Cecilia Thom
Cover: Joel Rojas
Cover pictures contributed by National Motor Museum/MPL, Tim Slade
Pictures contributed by ActionLibrary.com, LAT Photo,
National Motor Museum/MPL, SeriousWheels.com, Tim Slade

Printed and manufactured in China

Contents

What is it that attracts people to classic cars? Why bother spending so much time and money on old motor cars when you could have a perfectly good modern one, and enjoy clean fingernails and a healthy bank balance? Perhaps we need to start with the question - what exactly is a classic car? The obvious answer that most of us would come up with, is that a classic car is an old car. In fact the word 'classic' seems to have been commandeered just lately and redefined as an alternative for old. Of course the term 'classic' means far more than simply aged. It implies that something is, 'of the first rank or authority'. Plainly there is a lot more to this classic car thing than simply age. Does dodging the crusher for a few years really turn any car into a classic? Well, it's going to upset a few old car owners, but there is a bit more to it than that.

The cars that we've chosen for this book are pretty much all models that you are going to find it tough to argue against. It was no easy task to whittle down the tens of thousands of models built since Karl Benz took his three-wheeler onto the streets of Mannheim in 1885.

There are many different ways to earn the moniker 'classic', and for every car here, there is a different combination of all these reasons.

Breaking new ground is perhaps the most sure-fire way to earn your 'classic' status. The Mini, the Model T, the Beetle, the Citroen DS and even the Reliant Scimitar GTE can claim their place on this count. Providing reliable and much loved transport for vast numbers of people is another reason, claimed by the Model T and the Ford Cortina among other contenders.

Then there is the little matter of desire. The Duesenberg S and Mercedes 'K' cars appear to have been styled with little other than automotive lust in mind. The Mercedes 540K Special Roadster did such a good job that even so many decades later it still has much to do with our perception of the Mercedes brand.

What are the other factors that convey classic status? Performance alone is not enough, and there have been some ugly Ferraris and Lamborghinis that are beaten to the classic finishing line by the humble Fiat 500. Many cars sold well but failed entirely to generate affection in their owners. Generally these models have simply vanished. When did you last see an Austin Maxi or a Hillman Avenger? Even expensive cars went this way. What ever happened to all the Jaguar Mk Xs and Humber Super Snipes?

With cars having been around since 1885 it makes for an intriguing question to ask when the concept of the classic car might have first appeared delivered. And yet, at a time when the excitement and romance of the motor car was all

about the new, there is evidence that some motorists were already becoming attached to the old.

In October 1910 an article appeared in the British magazine *The Motor*, concerning a journey made in the car belonging to a friend of the author. The author claimed to have owned five different motor cars by this date, but his friend stuck with his first; a Benz from 1901. Even in 1910 this vehicle was considered an archaic contraption, and yet its owner professed many excellent reasons for preferring it to a more modern motor car. The solid tyres almost never wore out and, of course, there were no punctures to deal with. Another is that it travelled for 24 hilly miles on five pints of petrol – that's 38.4 miles to the gallon!

We have to wait until a few years later for the formalization of the 'things ain't what they used to be' ethos. It can be claimed with some authority that this came about in 1934, with the formation of the Vintage Sports Car Club, or VSCC. A group of enthusiasts met in a pub called the Phoenix at Hartley Wintney, a village about thirty miles west of London. They were there to discuss a proposition, in a now long-defunct magazine called *The Light Car*, that a club should be formed for the 'not so rich'. They were concerned that the heyday of historic motoring was coming to an end, and they felt that mass production was leading to quantity being considered more important than quality – arguments that are

The Humber Super Snipe may be an old car, but is it a classic car?

hard to quarrel with. And so they formed a club to encourage the use of cars built before 31 December 1930. Things were not all bad, and an approved list of modern cars was drawn up. The VSCC now welcomes cars from this list that were built up until 1941, as well as anything made before 1931.

The VSCC has endured and prospered, promoting racing and events for its members' cars, members will even get their cars out for the New Year's Day lunchtime gathering at the Phoenix, where you will see vintage Lagondas and Bentleys, whatever the weather and however much salt there is on the roads.

The very earliest motor cars are referred to as 'veteran'. All the cars built before December 1904 are veterans. These are the cars that are eligible for the UK's famous London to Brighton run. Cars built between 1905 and 1918 are properly called 'Edwardians'.

There are many and varied reasons to endure the rigours that are an unavoidable part of classic car ownership. The essential one is using the car. You could say that if a car isn't driven then it becomes something else – a work of art, a museum piece, a curio, a piece of junk, a waste of space or, perhaps, just forgotten. The essence of any motor car is in the driving – luckily this is a major motivation for most owners. A trip to the supermarket becomes a special event, and a sunny day is enough to provide an excuse for a drive. In London, for example, despite the traffic and terrible driving, it won't take long on a summer weekend before you see something special. It might be a Ferrari or a Morris 1000, but the enjoyment of using a classic is the same.

Held early in November every year, often in typically miserable English autumnal weather, there is always a good selection of registration plates from as far afield as the US and Australia. The number of cars taking part is something like a quite incredible 500. Some get little further than the gates of Hyde

Introduction

Park, London, where the run begins, but most make it to the seafront of Brighton. The event was first held in 1896 to celebrate that it had at last become legal for motor cars to be run upon English roads. The uniform 12mph speed limit, which seems very low, would not have been a major inconvenience at the time.

Held ever since, with breaks only for the two world wars, it's no surprise that it is the oldest consecutively held motoring event in the world.

The oldest competitive event, the Brighton Speed Trials, is held along the same stretch of road as the veteran's destination: Madeira Drive on Brighton seafront. It was first held in 1905, though due to disputes over the cost of resurfacing with the 'modern' tarmac it didn't happen again until 1923. Since 1932, it has only taken a break for the Second World War, and is still held every September. It is a fabulous place to see classics of all eras, on both two and four wheels, being given a real pasting.

All over the world there is historic racing taking place just about every summer weekend. In the US there are the legendary Monterey Historic Automobile Races at the Laguna Seca circuit in California. These events have grown in stature every year since the races were first held in 1974. Part of the same weekend is the Pebble Beach concours, where the finest and most fabulous classic cars compete for the honour of being the best and most beautiful in the world.

In the UK, it is the two events held at Goodwood that have captured everyone's imagination. A hill climb, or indeed a sprint, is an event where each car runs individually against the clock. First held in 1993, it instantly became a 'classic' in the old-car calendar.

Later in the summer the Goodwood Revival meeting takes place, held at the historic Goodwood circuit nearby. The first event was only held in 1998, and yet it has come to be generally regarded as the finest historic automotive event in the world. Racing is for pre-1966 cars – the year that contemporary racing stopped at Goodwood. The attention to the pre-'66 detail is terrific, and it has become the biggest fancy dress party in the world, as most race-goers arrive in period costume. Many also arrive with period transport – the special pre-'66 visitors' car park is one of the largest classic car meetings all on its own.

Curved Dash Oldsmobile

Like a phoenix from the flames, the Curved Dash Olds became the first mass-produced car

Ransom Eli Olds had been building experimental motor cars since 1887. By the 1890s, Olds had moved on to making gasoline-powered engines for use in factories and boats. It was in 1897 that he got serious about building motor cars, establishing the Olds Motor Vehicle Company. Then, in 1899, he moved the firm to the town that was to become known as 'Motor City' – Detroit.

A catastrophic fire in March 1901 destroyed all but one of Old's creations. He claimed that even the blueprints had been lost and that new ones had to be drawn up from the single survivor. This was to become the Curved Dash Oldsmobile and a runaway success.

With its premises in ruins, it was essential to get the car into production quickly to keep the company afloat. Olds made the clever decision to contract out the manufacture of his car's component parts: engines, transmissions and the skimpy little bodies were all made by other companies, and then assembled by Olds. He can be credited with single-handedly inventing the production line, with different groups of workers assembling the various parts of the vehicle.

The car had a wooden frame with long leaf springs running the length of it and providing front and rear suspension. High ground clearance meant it could cope with rough roads.

By the time production ceased in 1905, nearly 19,000 had been built. This made Oldsmobile the largest motor manufacturer in the world from 1903 to 1905. Many survive, and around 30 regularly take part in the London to Brighton run.

Specifications

Production dates	1901-1905
Manufactured units	18,525
Engine type	Single-cylinder, rear mounted
Engine size	1,565cc
Maximum power	5bhp
Transmission	2-speed epicyclic
Top speed	20mph
0-60 mph time	N/A
Country of origin	USA

Model T Ford

15 million Tin Lizzies put America and the world on wheels

In 1904, Henry Ford became the fastest man on earth when he drove his crude 'Arrow' across the frozen Lake St Clair at 91.37mph

In 1902, Ford stated his intention to 'build a car for the great multitudes'. By 1906, he was already America's largest

manufacturer, but the T was to revolutionize the industry.

Introduced in October 1908, it carried the rather hefty price tag of $850. Henry was under pressure to bring the price down, but refused to compromise on quality, so another way to reduce costs had to be found – and the answer came in the form of the world's first moving production line. Assembly time fell from 12 hours and 28 minutes to a remarkable 1 hour and 33 minutes. As production soared, the price dropped to an all-time low in 1925 – an extraordinarily cheap $290.

Ford paid his workers well and they worked hard as a result. Production numbers

were phenomenal, rising to nearly two million cars per year. The 'Tin Lizzie' lasted all the way through to 1927, by which time it had sold a fantastic 15,007,033 units.

The Model T changed little during its 19-year run. Model Ts were designed in a range of styles – from touring, runabout and coupé to two- and four-door sedans, not to mention delivery and commercial vehicles. Racing on banked board tracks was popular across the US, and Model Ts became a popular racer.

Specifications

Production dates	1908-1927
Manufactured units	15,007,033
Engine type	4-cylinder side-valve front-mounted
Engine size	2884cc
Maximum power	20bhp at 1,800rpm
Transmission	2-speed epicyclic
Top speed	42mph
0-60 mph time	N/A
Country of origin	USA

'Available in any shade – as long as it's black. Henry Ford found that black paint dried faster, speeding up production'

Austin Seven

Generations of British motorists learned to drive in the charming little Seven

Although primarily an engineer, Herbert Austin was no less an entrepreneur. By 1906, he had formed the Austin Motor Company, and by 1917 his famous factory at Longbridge was Britain's biggest motor works, due in part to large-scale war contracts. Austin was knighted for his services to the nation and became a Lord in 1936.

Austin implemented a single-model policy and a production line, but the large 20hp model was not a success. Austin escaped bankruptcy by merging with General Motors.

Deciding that cheaper cars were a safer bet, Austin introduced the Twelve in 1921, following it up in 1922 with the diminutive Seven. The Seven a small 747cc four-cylinder side-valve engine produced a modest 10bhp. This was set in a rather spindly A-shaped chassis.

It had four wheel brakes, but they were tiny and operated by stretchy cables. Its top speed was only 42mph.

The Seven appeared in many forms, including open tourers, two-seat convertibles, saloons and vans. There were also sporting models. The Seven went international, being built under licence in France, Germany and the US, but Americans were suspicious of such a tiny car and bankruptcy became inevitable.

Specifications

Production dates	1922-1939
Manufactured units	375,000+
Engine type	4-cylinder side-valve front-mounted
Engine size	747cc
Maximum power	10-14bhp (more for racing versions)
Transmission	early cars 3-speed; later cars 4-speed
Top speed	42mph
0-60 mph time	N/A
Country of origin	UK

'Swallow Sidecars built bodies for Austin Sevens that most definitely had ideas above their station. Swallow sidecars became SS, but of course after WW2 they changed their name to Jaguar'

Bentley 3.0 ltr

Famous victories at Le Mans for the Bentley Boys made the 3.0 ltr a legend

The Bentley was fairly conventional, even if its four-cylinder engine did have the modern configuration of four valves per cylinder operated by an overhead camshaft. This was mounted in a massively constructed chassis, and all of WO's four- and six-cylinder cars shared these features. Sales were slow at first and racing success was needed to promote the car. An entry into the inaugural Le Mans 24 Hour in 1923 netted fourth place. More success was to follow when

drivers Duff and Clement returned in 1924 with the new Speed Model and won.

Both 1925 and 1926 brought only retirements and so WO decided to develop a more powerful car – the 4.5-litre. 1927 is perhaps the most famous of all Le Mans 24 hours, and it was the 3.0-litre's finest hour. Three 3.0-litres and one 4.5-litre car were entered.

The big car took the lead, but three of the Bentleys became involved in a terrible six-car pile up

at White Horse corner. Miraculously, nobody was killed, and Sammy Davis managed to limp his 3.0-litre back to the pits.

There were further victories in the French race in 1928, 1929 and 1930, but they couldn't save Bentley from bankruptcy, and in 1931 the company was bought by Rolls Royce.

The 'Cricklewood' Bentleys remain the most archetypal of vintage cars, and more British than fish and chips or Buckingham Palace.

Specifications

Production dates	1921-1927
Manufactured units	1,633
Engine type	4-cylinder 16-valve front-mounted
Engine size	2,996cc
Maximum power	80-90 bhp
Transmission	4-speed
Top speed	80mph
0-60 mph time	N/A
Country of origin	UK

'At the 1927 Le Mans 24 hour race there was a terrible pile up at White House corner. The Bentley of Davis and Benjafield was involved, but somehow it limped back to the pits. Although it took half an hour to straighten out, it went on to score an heroic victory'

Bugatti Type 35/35B

The exquisite little blue cars from Molsheim won literally hundreds of races, including the first Monaco Grand Prix

Ettore Bugatti was an Italian who built the most celebrated cars ever to wear French racing blue. He set up in the town of Molsheim in Alsace and began trading on 1st January, 1910. His successful Brescia model, based on the pre-war Type 13, became a respected racing car, with many victories to its name.

In 1922, Ettore designed the engine for the Type 30 – a 2.0-litre straight eight with one exhaust and two inlet valves per cylinder, driven by an overhead camshaft. In 1924, a development of this engine was used to power the new Type 35 competition car. It was a Grand Prix car, but had two seats capable of carrying a riding mechanic.

Ettore created beautiful eight-spoke cast aluminium wheels, with integral brake drums. The engine was also a work of art, with a simple unadorned design.

The Type 35 was a huge success, and as it developed it became faster and faster. The Type 35B was the ultimate version, with a 2.3-litre engine fed by a supercharger. In 1926 it was capable of reaching 125mph, and in that year it won the World Championship. By the end of the 1920s Bugattis had won more races – including the first Monaco Grand Prix – than any other manufacturer, and Type 35Bs were credited with winning an average of 14 races per week

Today, the Type 35B is one of the world's most valuable cars – and if you've seen one racing, you'll know why. The music of the unsilenced straight eight, overlaid with the high-pitched scream of the supercharger, is never forgotten.

Specifications

Production dates	1926-1928
Manufactured units	45
Engine type	Straight 8 supercharged
Engine size	2,262cc
Maximum power	138bhp
Transmission	4-speed
Top speed	125mph
0-60 mph time	N/A
Country of origin	France

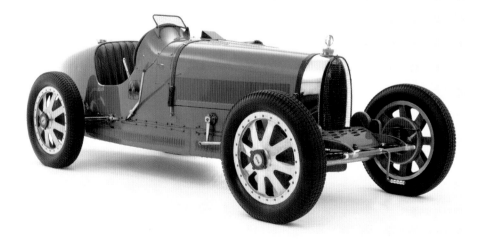

'The Type 35 and 35B Bugattis were phenomenally successful competition cars. In the late 1920s it was said that they averaged 14 race wins per week!'

Duesenberg Model J/SJ

*For Clarke Gable and Gary Cooper,
only a Duesenberg would do*

Fred and August Duesenberg's first road car was the Model A of 1920. It was expensive, but this was America's first straight eight, and the first with hydraulic brakes.

Unfortunately, the brothers went bust, and in 1926 the company was bought by entrepreneur Errett Cord, who owned Auburn. He released the Model J in December 1928.

Its engine was a 7.0-litre straight eight with four valves per cylinder and twin overhead camshafts, but it was four times the price of the most expensive Cadillac at the time.

The bodies were designed and built by the best coach builders, but Cord wanted a stronger, more individual identity, and so employed the gifted designer Gordon Buehrig. His fabulous designs were executed by coachbuilders such as Derham, Murphy, Brewster and Le Baron, and the results were some of the most opulent and extravagant automobiles ever seen.

This was not a great time to be selling expensive automobiles, as the Wall Street crash left few people able to afford them, but in 1932 the SJ was released. Only 36 people were rich enough to buy one. There was also a 400bph SSJ, bought only by movie stars.

Duesenbergs are the most treasured of all American cars, and on the rare occasions they change hands, it's usually behind closed doors for undisclosed – and unbelievable – sums of money.

Specifications

Production dates	1928-1935
Manufactured units	470
Engine type	Straight 8 twin cam DOHC; SJ/SSJ supercharged
Engine size	6,882cc
Maximum power	J 265bhp; SJ 320bhp; SSJ 400bhp
Transmission	4-speed
Top speed	J 115mph; SJ 140mph
0-60 mph time	J 8.6 seconds
Country of origin	USA

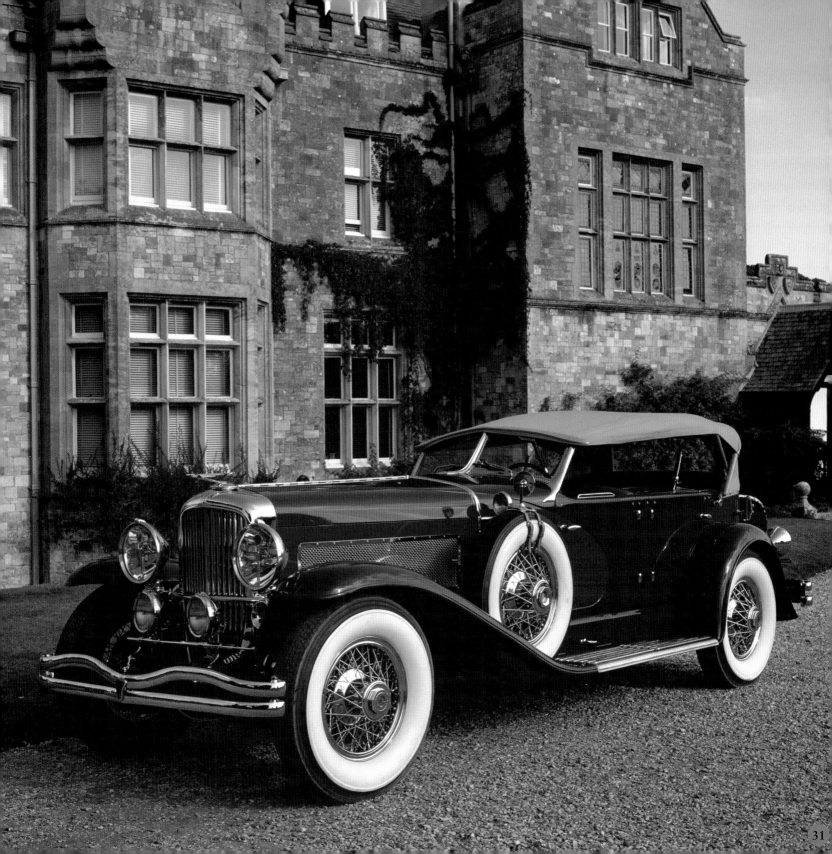

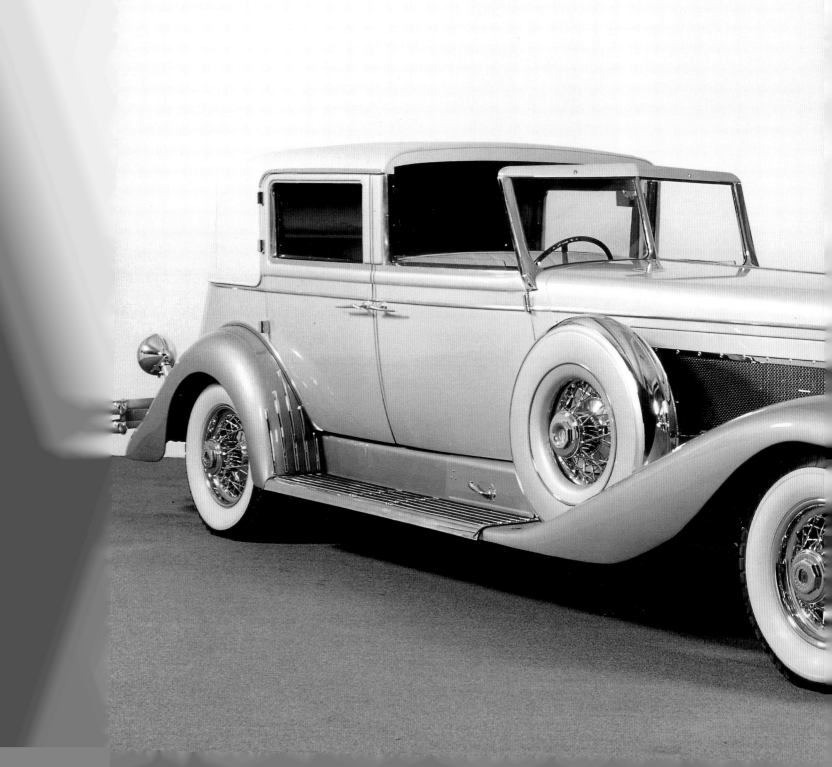

'The Model J Duesenbergs
were the most fabulous
American cars ever made - and
so they should have been, as
they were the highest priced
cars in the world'

'32 Ford

With his first V8 Henry Ford really did bring power to the people

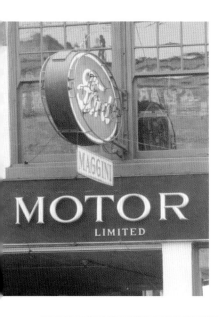

After 15,000,000 Tin Lizzies came the Model A. Within 18 months of its 1928 launch, there were 2,000,000 of them on America's roads. It had a four cylinder engine, and although a little dearer, Chevrolet could give you six

Ford engineers had been working on a low cost V8 engine, released on April 2nd 1932, there were 14 V8 models to choose from. The styling was sleek, modern and very attractive. With an 80mph top speed they were faster than most sports cars. Ford won back sales from the competition, but the Depression meant that only 232,125 cars were built in 1932.

The 3,621cc side valve engine had huge tuning potential, and it was the 1932, or 'Deuce', which got hot rodding going all on its own. A few stripped-out, hopped-up '32s would make their way to the dry lake beds in California for illegal races. When GIs returned after WW2, the Deuce was a cheap way to go fast, and the whole hot rod and drag racing scene took off.

Specifications

Production dates	1932
Manufactured units	232,125
Engine type	side valve V8
Engine size	3,621cc
Maximum power	65bhp
Transmission	3-speed synchromesh
Top speed	80mph
0-50 mph time	12 seconds
Country of origin	USA

Mercedes 500K/540K

Charismatic or caricature; the K cars were the ultimate embodiment of 1930s style

The Mercedes marque had become associated with supercharging in the late 1920s with the mighty SS and SSK sports cars. These were stripped down racers where form obeyed function – something that could never be said of the K cars.

The 500K was built to be magnificent. Its 5.0-litre engine was moved 7in back in the chassis to allow the radiator grill to be set right back behind the axle line. The bonnet was impossibly long, though this was partially excused by the length of that engine. There were many body styles, designed and built in-house at Sindlefingen, and all were breathtaking. Performance was good, but not quite up to expectations.

In 1936 came the 540K with 180bhp. This was produced only when the supercharger was engaged, which could be done only in short bursts. It was renowned for making a fearsome scream, although there are those who say that this had more to do with the perception of increased performance than any extra horse power involved. With that blower going, fuel consumption dropped to just 8mpg!

Unusually for exclusive cars of the time, nearly all of the K cars were bodied at the factory. The four-seater cabriolet B and the two-seater cabriolet A are highly prized, but the Special Roadster is the supreme embodiment. It has more curves and chrome than almost any car in history; the epitome of 'erotic' aesthetics in car design.

Specifications

Production dates	500K 1934-1936 540K 1936-1939
Manufactured units	500K 354; 540K 406
Engine type	straight eight OHV supercharged
Engine size	500K 5,018cc; 540K 54,01cc
Maximum power	(with supercharger) 500K 160bhp; 540K 180bhp
Transmission	3 speed + overdrive / 4 speed / 4 speed +
Top speed	105mph
0-50 mph time	16 seconds
Country of origin	Germany

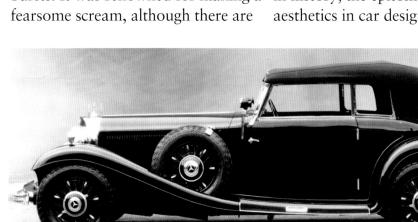

'Even when clothed in coachwork that was relatively restrained, and wearing sombre black paintwork, the 'K' cars could manage a flamboyance that few could approach'

Auburn 851/ 852 Speedster

Genius Buehrig's makeover creates an all-time classic design

Errett Lobban Cord had made and lost his fortune three times over by the age of 24, but by 1924, his genius for selling seemed to have cemented his wealth. Taken on to run the ailing Auburn company, he immediately spruced up the unsold cars with jazzy colors – and, sure enough, they sold. He soon bought the company, becoming its dynamic president in 1926 at the age of 32.

A new Auburn range was introduced, the most important being a straight eight. The engine was built by aero engine makers Lycoming, which Cord had also bought. In fact, by 1929 his Cord Corporation controlled over 150 companies!

In 1928 came the Speedster. In 1934, the Speedster received a makeover, but it wasn't enough. What the Speedster needed was a complete redesign, but unfortunately there simply wasn't the money for an all-new car.

The young designer Gordon Buehrig had been doing amazing work for the Cord Corporation, including creating the 'Duesenberg look'. Given the job of sorting out the Speedster, but with 100 bodies in stock needing to be used up, his redesign could only be superficial.

Taking the 1928 car he created a new rear end, hood, grill and fenders. With this he managed to fashion what appeared to be a completely new car, and one of the all time great automotive shapes. It was introduced in 1935 as the 851, and then again in 1936 as the 852, although little more than the badge had changed between the two.

The 851's simple side valve straight eight was supercharged to 150bhp, but it was essentially a cheap car in a fancy suit.

Specifications

Production dates	851 1935; 852 1936-1937
Manufactured units	851/852 all styles 6,850; Speedster approx 600
Engine type	straight eight supercharged
Engine size	4,585cc
Maximum power	150bhp
Transmission	3-speed + 2-speed (6-speed)
Top speed	103mph
0-50 mph time	15 seconds
Country of origin	USA

'Buehrig managed to fashion what appeared to be a completely new car, and one of the all-time great automotive shapes'

Rolls-Royce Phantom III

The last word in 1930s bespoke engineering

The 'best cars in the world' came about through the partnership of engineer Henry Royce and salesman Charles Rolls. Their 40/50 model of 1906, known as the Silver Ghost, was certainly worthy of this accolade: the famously silent Ghost was made right up until 1926, with many built at their US factory in Springfield, Massachusetts.

In 1926 came the Phantom I, with a new overhead valve 7,668cc six-cylinder engine. For 1929 it evolved into the Phantom II. There was also a smaller 20hp model, which developed into the 20/25 and the 25/30. It was the Phantom III, however, that was to be the pinnacle of pre-WW2 automotive engineering.

The aircraft and ship engines produced by Rolls-Royce were a major influence on the engine of the PIII, a 7,340cc overhead valve V12. Cadillac had tried to go one up with a V16, but it was a simple side-valve device, and not in the same engineering league as the PIII. The advantages of the V12 layout were sublime smoothness and considerable power: Rolls-Royce were always coy about power outputs, simply stating that they were 'adequate'. In fact, the V12 made something like 170bhp, which was more than adequate.

The PIII also had far more modern suspension than its predecessors. The independent front suspension used coil springs and wishbones, that were developed by General Motors.

Hostilities of 1939 halted production, which meant that the V12 never reached its development potential, and the era of hand-built bespoke engineering came to a close.

Specifications

Production dates	1936-1939
Manufactured units	710
Engine type	V12, pushrod operated overhead valve
Engine size	7,340cc
Maximum power	170bph
Transmission	4-speed synchromesh
Top speed	Approx 92mph
0-50 mph time	N/A
Country of origin	UK

Cord 810/812

*The streamlined Cord car and Cord
the man: both American icons*

Having bought and turned around both Auburn and Duesenberg, in 1929 Cord launched his own car. The Cord L-29 was radical in that it had front wheel drive. The Miller front-drive racing cars had been beating the Duesenbergs at Indianapolis, and Cord wanted it for his road car.

In December 1935, the new Cord 810 debuted at the New York show. It was a sensation.

There was still front wheel drive, but a far more sophisticated design. There was a also a new V8 engine, with the option of supercharging up to 190bhp, pushing the Cord to 110 mph.

Designer Gordon Buehrig had created a stylish masterpiece. Construction was unitary, with no separate chassis, which allowed the car to be very low to the ground. Headlights were hidden in the fenders, while louvers extended round the front and back to the doors, with a 'coffin nose' hood above. The interior was also spectacular, with an aircraft-inspired dashboard. Convertible, phaeton and two sedan models were constructed.

Unusually, it is the sedans that are the most stunning, with lines that were cleaner than anything on American or European roads at the time.

For 1937, the Cords were retitled 812s. It was to be their last year. Cord had gone to England in 1934 due to investigations into his business practices. In 1937, a bill was filed against him, which meant that Cord production stopped.

These were hard times in the US, and sales of the revolutionary Cord were never strong, but Buehrig's shape is now recognized as one of the most beautiful and influential automotive designs of all time.

Specifications

Production dates	1936-1937
Manufactured units	2,320
Engine type	V8 side-valve, optional supercharger
Engine size	4,719cc
Maximum power	115bhp (190bhp supercharged)
Transmission	4-speed, electric gear selection, front wheel drive
Top speed	91mph (110mph supercharged)
0-50 mph time	N/A
Country of origin	USA

'Designer Gordon Buehrig gave the Cord some of the most original and beautiful lines ever seen. It was no less imaginative under the skin, with front wheel drive and electric gear selection'

Jeep

The GIs' transport of choice that went from being a legend to an institution

Bantam had been making Austin Sevens under licence, but were not doing well. They enlisted freelance engineer Karl K Probst, and a prototype and drawings were duly delivered in an incredible seven weeks. Although overweight, it was considered to

be a success. Ford and Willys Overland also submitted. They had access to the Bantam, and so their designs were very similar.

The Willys had the best engine. The design was standardized, and due to concerns about Bantam's lack of capacity, the contract eventually went to Willys.

America entered the war and demand soared. At their peak, a Jeep was leaving the Willys production line every 90 seconds. By the end of the war, over 350,000 Jeeps had been supplied to US,

British and Russian forces. The Jeep's 60bhp side-valve four-cylinder engine gave it a top speed of over 60mph. With minimal overhangs and good ground clearance, it took seriously rough terrain to halt its progress, and ended up being used as everything from a gun platform, to radio car, reconnaissance vehicle and ambulance. It was easy to drive, simple to maintain, and extremely tough.

Willys went on to build a civilian version, others copied the formula, and the British Land Rover went on sale as early as 1948.

Specifications

Production dates	1941 to present
Manufactured units	1941-1945 350,000
Engine type	4-cylinder side valve
Engine size	2199cc
Maximum power	60bhp
Transmission	3-speed sychromesh + 2-speed transfer box, 4-wheel drive
Top speed	65mph
0-50 mph time	N/A
Country of origin	USA

'In the Jeep was a rightness found only when form follows function and purpose so completely. A very similar vehicle to the WW2 Jeep is still made in India'

MG TC

Old-fashioned and not very fast, but post-war America fell in love with the little MG

The first MGs appeared in 1929, MG really got moving with the Midget. Based on the Morris Minor, it had a lively and modern overhead cam 850cc engine.

In 1930, 1,000 MGs were built, this was also the year that the famous slogan, 'safety fast', was coined. MGs were doing well on the race tracks, beating arch rivals Austin in the Brooklands Double Twelve – Britain's equivalent of the Le Mans 24 Hour – amongst many other victories.

1933 saw the creation of the J2 Midget, and this was to establish the styling of MGs all the way through to the 1950s: a radiator well set back, flowing wings, cut down doors, a fuel tank on the back and a folding windscreen.

In 1934 came the TA Midget, which was based on the Morris Ten saloon, and which used its pushrod 1,292cc engine. The engine was more flexible, and, with softer suspension and modern hydraulic brakes, it was an altogether easier

car to drive. The traditional MG styling had reached its perfection, and it is still many people's idea of what a real sports car should be.

After 1945, there was a huge hunger for new cars, in 1946, thousands of units went to America, starting the US love affair with British sports cars that has endured to this day.

Specifications

Production dates	1946-1949
Manufactured units	10,000
Engine type	4-cylinder pushrod OHV
Engine size	1,250cc
Maximum power	54bhp
Transmission	4-speed synchromesh
Top speed	78mph
0-50 mph time	N/A
Country of origin	UK

'These were the vehicles that started the US' enduring love affair with British sports cars'

VW Beetle

The inimitable Bug has the strangest and longest story of any motor car in history

On July 30th, 2003, Beetle number 21,529,464 left the Puebla factory in Mexico. It was the very last one. The story of the world's most successful car had started an incredible 70 years earlier – and it's one of the most remarkable business.

Hitler is often credited with inventing the Beetle, but it wasn't really so. The idea came from Dr Ferdinand Porsche, and was brought to Hitler's attention in 1933, the year that he became chancellor. It was on June 22, 1934 that Porsche secured a contract to build a prototype for the 'people's car'.

With assistance from Mercedes Benz, three cars were built in 1936, and a further 30 pre-production cars in 1937. In 1938, Hitler laid the foundation stone of the factory near Hanover, where the car, called 'KdF-Wagen', was to be built.

The factory, and the town built to service it, ended up under the jurisdiction of the British Military Government. A young Major Ivan Hirst was appointed to sort out the factory, which had last been used to build rockets with slave labour, and which had been badly bombed. Hirst saw the potential, and persuaded the military police to place an order for 20,000 vehicles.

VW promoted the little car in the US, and against all preconceptions the Americans took the Bug to their heart, buying them in their millions.

Specifications

Production dates	1946-2003
Manufactured units	21,529,464
Engine type	Flat 4, air-cooled, rear-mounted
Engine size	1131cc-1584cc
Maximum power	25bhp-50bhp
Transmission	4-speed synchromesh
Top speed	62mph-82mph
0-60 mph time	17.1 seconds (1303-1584cc)
Country of origin	Germany

'...against all preconceptions the Americans took the Bug to their heart, buying them in their millions'

Hudson Hornet

Race track domination and fabulous looks couldn't save Hudson

Hudson had been around since 1908 and, at times in the 1930s, had risen as high as number five in US sales, but remained a relatively small fish in an extremely big pond, and so life was never easy, they made enough cars to regain fifth place. The cars created between 1945 and 1947 were based on old designs, but for 1948 it had an all-new car. These were the 'Step Down' Hudsons, and the Commodore models made money for the old firm.

The Hornet looked much like the Commodore, but with a new grill. Marshall Teague said he could get 112mph out of a car certified as stock by the racing authorities. The Hudson engineers developed 'severe usage' parts, which were really racing equipment. In 1953, the Twin H Power carburettor setup was offered. The ultimate '7-X' racing engine could make 210bhp.

Teague raced the Hornet in AAA and NASCAR stock-car events from 1951 and was simply invincible through to 1954, winning 12 out of 13 races in the 1952 AAA season.

As late as 1955, after Step Down production had finished, the Hornet was still winning races.

The trouble was that the Hornet's modern unitary construction and fabulous lines made it impossible to restyle year to year in the way that most manufacturers did: all its designers could do was fiddle with the trim. The 1955 Hudson used a Nash body, and was disparagingly referred to as a 'Hash'.

Specifications

Production dates	1951-1953
Manufactured units	106,785
Engine type	6-cylinder side valve
Engine size	5,048cc
Maximum power	145bhp, Twin H Power 160bhp
Transmission	3-speed manual, with options of overdrive and Drive-Master semi automatic. Hydra-Matic automatic gearbox optional
Top speed	105mph
0-60 mph time	12-14 seconds
Country of origin	USA

Mercedes 300SL

Could the 300SL be the world's most desired automobile?

The new car was a sensation, winning both Le Mans and the Carrera Panamericana in 1952. It was called the 300SL, but it

was only a racing car – and that's the way it would have stayed if it hadn't been for New York car importer Max Hoffmann, who saw the potential of the 300SL as a road car in the US. The factory wasn't really interested until Hoffmann made a firm order for 1,000 cars.

In 1954, the 300SL became a road car. Where the racer had been aerodynamic but ugly, the road car was stunning. It kept the upward opening doors of the racer, and this led to its being universally called the 'Gullwing'.

It was the first road car with a fuel-injected engine, and with 195bhp it could top 150mph with a high ratio axle. However, this gem was not without its

flaws: the suspension was taken from the 300 saloon, and at the back used a very old-fashioned swing axle design. This could cause a sudden breakaway, and the Gullwing killed a fair few drivers with more money than ability.

In 1957, the Gullwing gave way to the Roadster, which had large, one-piece headlights and regular doors. Most importantly, the rear suspension had been redesigned and the handling improved.

The 300SL created the SL tradition that lasts to this day, with the cars themselves more desirable now than at any point in their formidable history.

Specifications

Production dates	1954-1957 (Gullwing); 1957-1963 (Roadster)
Manufactured units	1,400 (Gullwing); 1,858 (Roadster)
Engine type	Straight 6 single overhead cam, fuel-injected
Engine size	2,996cc
Maximum power	195bhp (Gullwing); 215bhp (Roadster)
Transmission	4-speed
Top speed	125mph-150mph
0-60 mph time	7-9 seconds, dependent on final drive ratio
Country of origin	Germany

'Values for the Gullwing are higher than for the Roadster, due to its overt racing heritage. In fact the Roadster is better to drive, just as fast, and you don't have to lift out the windows to keep cool!'

Citroen DS

Spaceship or goddess; to many the DS was both

The DS and cheaper ID shared a rather old-fashioned engine, and had the engine behind the

gearbox as had been seen in the Traction Avant, but everything else was new.

The car's life blood was its high-pressure hydraulic system. There were no steel springs and the suspension gave an unworldly soft ride, plus there was also the ability to adjust the ride height, although the DS's party trick was its ability to drive on three wheels (which allowed drivers to change a wheel without a jack). The brake pedal was a button, the sensitivity of which caught out every novice driver first time, while the power steering utilised hydraulics, and some models even had hydraulic gear and clutch engagement (although the simpler ID boasted only the suspension and braking systems).

Specifications

Production dates	1955-1975
Manufactured units	1,456,115
Engine type	4-cylinder push rod OHV
Engine size	1,911cc; 1,985cc; 2,175cc; 2,347cc
Maximum power	109bhp (DS21)
Transmission	4-manual and semi-automatic, front-wheel drive
Top speed	106mph (DS21)
0-60 mph time	14.8 seconds (DS21)
Country of origin	France

As time went by, its designers came up with increases in power and sophistication, such as swivelling head lights. Later models were designated the DS20, DS21 and DS23. The Pallas, meanwhile, was a luxury model, the Safari was a cavernous estate, and there was even a coupé and a convertible by Chapron, both highly prized collectors' items with prices to match.

On the DS's 50th anniversary, Paris ground to a halt as thousands of DSs came to celebrate their birthday.

'Though most DSs provided everyday transport for the French middle classes, the convertible by Chapron was something rare and special. Today these wear a price tag that is truly exclusive'

'55-'57 Ford Thunderbird

For the T-Bird, first was best, as the purity of the two-seater cars was never fully recaptured

It was Chevrolet that made the Thunderbird happen. In 1953, it brought out the Corvette, and GM certainly weren't going to have anything that Ford didn't have

The T-Bird fused low-slung elegance with a thoroughly Ford look. It was not the out-and-out sports car that the early Corvette had tried and failed to be. It sat on the same 102in wheelbase, but there were proper wind-up windows, a power top and a lift-off hard top. Under the hood was a beefy 193bhp Mercury V8, while the 'Vette struggled with flappy side screens and a limp six pot. Under that gorgeous skin it might have run on standard Ford parts from lesser models in the range, but who cared?

Detroit restyled its models every season in the 1950s, but the runaway success of the T-Bird meant that it was too good to change. For 1957 there was a light makeover, with a different bumper and grill, and a longer rear deck for more trunk space. Elegance was undiminished, and you could now get up to 285bhp if you ticked the right boxes. They even went racing with a 340bhp supercharged version – only 208 were built, and success was limited.

Ford wanted greater sales, and for 1958 the T-Bird became a four seater.

Specifications

Production dates	1955-1957
Manufactured units	53,166
Engine type	V8 pushrod OHV
Engine size	4,785cc; 5,112cc
Maximum power	193bhp-285bhp
Transmission	3-speed manual with optional overdrive, or 3-speed automatic
Top speed	105mph-125mph
0-60 mph time	11.5-7.0 seconds
Country of origin	USA

*'...the runaway success of
the T-Bird meant that it
was too good to change'*

'55, '56, '57 Chevrolets

Few cars have been as right as the '55 Chevy with its new V8. Except perhaps the '57

The '54 Chevy was upright, old fashioned and had a dull six under the hood. The all-new '55 Chevy, on the other hand, could not have been more different. 1955 saw the birth of the 'Small Block' V8, super-modern in design and built for high revs and low weight.

There were two- and four-door cars, a four-door station wagon, a convertible, and three ranges – the One-Ten, Two-Ten, and the desirable Bel Air. Then there was the Nomad: a station wagon styling exercise on the Corvette was so well received at shows that the design was rapidly adapted for the '55 model. The two-door wagon was stunning: it cost more than the convertible and sold slowly, but Tri Chevy Nomads remain a collector's dream.

For 1956, there was a gentle restyle, and the pillarless two-door car was joined by a 'hard top' four-door pillarless sedan. The restyle was successful, but today the '56 is less sought after than its '55 and '57 cousins.

In 1957, Chevy gave the option of fuel injection – a first on an American car, and not so far behind Mercedes Benz with the 300SL. It made 283bhp and blasted the '57 to 60 in eight seconds, but cost a whopping $500, so only 1,503 'Fuelies' got built.

No cars better epitomise the decade than the Tri Chevys.

Specifications

Production dates	1955, 1956, 1957
Manufactured units	'55 1,703,993
	'56 1,563,729
	'57 1,499,658
Engine type	straight 6 and V8 OHV
Engine size	straight 6 3,850 cc;
	V8 4,342cc/4,637cc
Maximum power	(V8) 162bhp-283bhp
Transmission	3-speed manual with optional overdrive, or 2-speed automatic
Top speed	(V8) 90mph-120mph
0-60 mph time	(V8) 11.4-8.0 seconds
Country of origin	USA

'The '57 was the last of the "Tri Chevys" and in two-door Bel Air hardtop form, as here, it has a perfection of line that you just can't knock'

Aston Martin DB4/DB5

The DB Astons were the epitome of the post-war sports car.

Specifications

Production dates	1958-1963 (DB4); 1963-1965 (DB5)
Manufactured units	1,110 (DB4); 1,021 (DB5)
Engine type	Twin-cam 6-cylinder
Engine size	3,670cc (DB4); 3,995cc (DB5)
Maximum power	240bhp (DB4); 285bhp (DB5); 315bph (DB4 Zagato)
Transmission	4-speed sychromesh
Top speed	140mph+
0-60 mph time	8.1 seconds
Country of origin	UK

The DB2 of 1949 was a sleek coupé along the lines of Ferraris at the time. Rather confusingly, it developed to become the DB2/4, DB2/4 Mk II, and the DB Mk III. The DB3 was a sports racing car, as were the DB3S and the DBR 1, which won both Le Mans and the World Sports Car Championship for David Brown in 1959.

The DB4 in 1958 was all new, including its engine, designed by Polish engineer Tadek Marek. It was another twin-cam six, but larger at 3,670cc. It was claimed to make 240bhp, and to give the DB4 a top speed of 140mph, both claims that may have been a little enthusiastic.

The styling was svelte and lithe, and the unique bodywork was handmade using the 'superleggera', or 'super light', technique of Carrozzeria Touring of Milan.

In 1962 there came a convertible. There was a faster Vantage version, and a very fast short wheelbase DB4 GT. Then there were 19 GTs with beautiful bodies built by Zagato in Italy. In 1963 the DB4 became the DB5. It used the faired-in lights of the GT, but looked little different to the DB4.

'The Aston Martin DB4 sets the gold standard for classics. Beautiful, fast, rare and, above all, utterly desirable'

Facel Vega HK500

The exotic HK500 never quite fitted in, but remains one of the most romantic cars ever made

In the early 1950s, the Facel company of wealthy industrialist Jean Daninos was making everything from kitchen sinks to jet engine parts. Then it started making bodies for auto makers such as Simca, Panhard and Ford. The French Ford Comete of 1952 was a pretty coupé, but Daninos wanted to build his own car.

In 1954 he presented the Facel Vega FVS. Powered by one of the best engines of the day, the Chrysler 'Hemi' V8, it was fast and very beautiful. Its styling was truly 'transatlantic', with an unmistakable American influence filtered through European sensibilities, while the wrap-around windscreen and forward lean gave it a unique look. The Facel was the first of several British and Italian–American hybrids, but none achieved the perfect fusion of styles seen in the Facel.

A stretched four-door FVS called the Excellence arrived in 1958. With pillarless construction and suicide rear doors it looked incredible, but unfortunately it wasn't rigid enough, and if parked on anything other than a flat surface, the doors would refuse to open.

In 1959 the FVS became the HK500, with an even bigger 5,907cc Chrysler V8, while later cars had a 6,286cc engine with up to 390bhp! Unfortunately, the chassis wasn't really up to it, the steering said to be 'vega' than most. The styling was perfected, and the cars were equally spectacular on the inside. The aircraft style wrap-around dashboard appeared to be in heavily figured burr walnut, but in fact it was steel, painted by a talented tromp l'oeil artist.

In 1962 came the Facel II, with a totally different look. The big V8 cars were always slow sellers, but it was Daninos' ill-fated venture building his own small sports-car engine that eventually sank the company.

Specifications

Production dates	1959-1961
Manufactured units	500
Engine type	V8 Hemi
Engine size	5,907cc; 6,286 cc
Maximum power	325bhp-390bhp
Transmission	4-speed manual or automatic
Top speed	140+ mph
0-60 mph time	8.4 seconds
Country of origin	France

Jaguar Mk II

Beloved of both bank managers and bank robbers, the Mk II is still the greatest Jaguar saloon

William Lyons and William Walmsley set up their Swallow Sidecars business in 1922. By 1927, they had progressed to building bodies on Austin Seven chassis. They looked extravagant but were keenly priced, and sold well. In 1931 came their first proper car: the SS. In 1935, a new six-cylinder saloon and sports car were launched, both called the SS Jaguar. The cars looked to be in the same class as Bentleys, but at a quarter of the price.

There was soon a new Jaguar engine on the block. This was the legendary twin overhead cam, six-cylinder XK unit. It powered both the XK sports cars and the Mk VII, VIII and IX saloons. These were big cars, but the XK engine gave them with remarkable performance.

Something sportier was needed, and in 1955 the much smaller Mk I was released. With the same 3.4-litre engine as its big brother, it was considerably quicker. It was an instant hit, but when Jaguar developed it into the Mk II in 1959, it created its most famous saloon ever.

The Mk II dominated the new production saloon racing, but there were other, less salubrious characters who also appreciated its performance. The Mk II became infamous as the bank robber's getaway car of choice, and no self-respecting 1960s cop drama was complete without a tyre-smoking Mk II.

Specifications

Production dates	1959-1967
Manufactured units	83,976
Engine type	Twin overhead cam 6-cylinder
Engine size	2,483cc; 3,442cc; 3,781cc
Maximum power	120bhp; 210bhp; 220bhp
Transmission	4-speed with optional overdrive
Top speed	125mph (3.8)
0-60 mph time	8.5 seconds (3.8)
Country of origin	UK

'The Mk II was formidable on the track. Seen here cresting Paddock Hill and braking for Druids corner at Brands Hatch, the "BUY 12" registration gives the white car away as a 'Coombes' Jaguar, from John Coombes garage in Guildford'

Austin-Healey Sprite

If ever a car proved that you don't have to go fast to have fun, it was the 'Frogeye'

Donald Healey had worked for various British car makers before and during WW2, and in 1945 was quick to acquire a factory in Warwick, England.

In the early 1950s, boss of BMC Sir Leonard Lord, which included both Austin and Morris, was on the lookout for a sports-car design. He liked what

Healey showed him and the Healey 100 was the result. Meanwhile, Healey was happy because he didn't have to build the cars!

The 100 gained a six-cylinder engine, becoming the 100/6 and later the 3000. In the mid-1950s there was a gap in the market for a small, no-frills sports car, and Healey was asked to develop one: the Austin-Healey Sprite of 1958. Charm it had aplenty, and although its top speed was only 83mph, it was a hoot to drive.

The little 948cc A-Series engine

from the Austin A35 saloon had a lively and eager character quite at odds with its humble specification. The front suspension also came from the little Austin, but 1/4 elliptic rear springs located the axle much better. A more conventional restyle came in 1961, and the Sprite was joined by the near-identical MG Midget.

Engines got bigger and weight increased. The last Sprite was made in 1971, but the Midget soldiered on until 1980, by which time it was a rather overweight shadow of the first original Sprite.

Specifications

Production dates	1959-1961
Manufactured units	48,987
Engine type	4-cylinder push rod OHV
Engine size	948cc
Maximum power	43bhp
Transmission	4-speed, synchromesh on top 3 gears
Top speed	83mph
0-60 mph time	18 seconds
Country of origin	UK

Cadillac

In the 1950s, the American dream had come true, and the '59 was perhaps its ultimate manifestation

Has there ever been a car so famed for just one feature? With the '59 Caddies it was all about those fins. For 1960 they'd been trimmed back, and by 1965 fins were just a memory for the American auto industry.

It was all their fault in the first place.

Harley Earl, or 'Misterearl', as he was always referred to, had pretty much come up with the idea of car styling. At General Motors in 1925 he introduced the concept of annual model changes and – although he wouldn't have put it this way – designed obsolescence. When GM formed its Art and Colour section in 1927, Earl was in charge. It started with 50 people, but was to grow to 1,400. Back in 1941, Earl had seen the still secret P38 Lightning fighter plane. He took the beautiful tail fin shape and applied it to his '48 Cadillacs.

Throughout the 1950s, US styling grew more outrageous. There were some biggies on Chryslers and Plymouths, but the '59 Caddie's beat them all. With twin bullet lights mounted half way up, looking like small rockets, style had completely triumphed over function. The '59 wasn't even a very good car, but no-one noticed. It had a V8 under the hood, like any other Cadillac, but no-one asked any questions. Sure, the front end suffered from vibration and it handled badly. So what?

Specifications

Production dates	1959
Manufactured units	142,272
Engine type	V8 OHV
Engine size	6390cc
Maximum power	325/345bhp
Transmission	Hydra-Matic auto
Top speed	120mph
0-60 mph time	11.5
Country of origin	USA

ultimate icon
Americana'

Mini

The Mini put more new ideas into 10ft than had ever been seen in one car before

Alex Issigonis was a genuine genius. During the fuel crisis of 1956, he put his extraordinary mind to creating a new sort of small car – and no small car has

been packaged as well as the Mini. His first big idea was to turn the engine across the car. Most cars have transverse engines these days, but the Mini was the first. Then he put the gearbox under the engine, in its sump. This meant them sharing their oil, but developments in lubrication meant this wasn't a problem.

The suspension used rubber for springs, which saved space again. Issigonis didn't like wasting space on a boot that was seldom used, so the lid to the tiny boot opened downwards, and larger loads could be carried with the boot open. This left more room for passengers, and the Mini was something of a

Tardis. To make manufacture cheaper, the body's seams were turned outwards, welded together and covered with trim.

The Mini came as a van, a pickup, and a Traveller estate with wood trim. There were luxury Riley Elf and Wolseley Hornet versions, and later the Clubman and 1,275GT. Its unique status meant it looked as though it would last forever, but time was finally called on October 4th 2000, when the last Mini rolled off the production line.

Specifications

Production dates	1959-2000
Manufactured units	5,387,862
Engine type	4-cylinder transverse
Engine size	848cc-1,275cc
Maximum power	34bhp-76bhp
Transmission	4-speed in sump
Top speed	72mph-96mph
0-60 mph time	29.7-10.5 seconds
Country of origin	UK

JUY 232D

Ferrari 250G SWB

No other car has combined everyday roadability and weekend track talent like the SWB

In 1928, Enzo Ferrari founded Scuderia Ferrari, a racing team competing in the fabulous Alfa Romeo racing cars of the time. He built a couple of cars in 1940, but the Ferrari name didn't appear on a car until after WW2. The first Ferrari appeared in 1946 with a 2.0-litre V12 engine designed by the great Gioacchino Columbo, and was winning races by 1947.

The first road cars came a year later, powered by versions of the V12. The trouble was that Enzo was giving his attention to winning Grand Prix. They lifted the World Championship in 1952, 1953, and 1958, with further titles in 1961 and 1964. They also won Le Mans in 1949, 1954, 1958, 1960 and 1965.

A short chassis development appeared in 1960, and the 250GT Short Wheel Base Berlinetta was born. Bodywork was styled by Pininfarina and built by Scaglietti. You could have it in steel or aluminium, and no two cars were exactly the same. Production-car racing was very popular, and the 250SWB was the car to drive if you wanted to win. What was unique about the SWB was that it really could be driven to the shops, then driven to the track, raced, and driven home again.

Specifications

Production dates	1960-1962
Manufactured units	165
Engine type	60-degree V12
Engine size	2,953cc
Maximum power	220bhp-280bhp
Transmission	4-speed synchromesh
Top speed	145mph-155mph
0-60 mph time	6.3 seconds
Country of origin	Italy

'The GTO may be more famous, but the SWB is still the greatest dual-purpose car ever built'

Mercedes Benz 180

The 180 made Mercedes a major manufacturer.
But is it a classic...?

After WW2 Daimler Benz started building a small pre-war model, and it proved to be its salvation. In 1953 came the 180. It was simply styled, perhaps even a little dumpy. The engine and front suspension was carried on a separate subframe – a little like a pontoon bridge. Volvo claims to have pioneered crumple zones but, in fact, the 180 was the first car to incorporate the concept.

Engines were the slow, wheezy, diesel, and side-valve petrol units from the old 170. Not until 1957 did the 180 get a detuned version of the overhead cam engine from the 190SL, and decent performance.

On these journeys it cruised at 75mph, even though the top speed is only 84mph. There have been one or two problems, but nothing that stopped it from getting home. Just to prove that using an old car doesn't do it any harm, it has also won its class in the Mercedes Benz Club national concours.

Specifications

Production dates	1953196262 (189b 1959-1961)
Manufactured units	271,217 (all types)
Engine type	4-cylinder petrol, OHC (180b)
Engine size	1,897cc (180b)
Maximum power	68bhp (180b)
Transmission	4-speed synchromesh, column change
Top speed	84mph
0-60 mph time	18 seconds
Country of origin	Germany

Jaguar E-Type

America loved it so much that they bought most of them

First there had been the C-Type, with the brand new technology of disc brakes. Then came the D-Type with its aerodynamic form and unitary chassis. All the lessons learnt at the La Sarthe track were

used in the design of the E-Type.

There were Dunlop disc brakes all round, and the body was of unitary, or monocoque, construction. This allowed it to be low, and it's hard to think of a car that looks lower than the E-Type. It plainly owed much to the lines of the D-Type, but that was a racing car and didn't have to sell. The E-Type shared the same small oval grill and faired-in lights, but it was styled to please – and please it did. The roadster and the fixed-head coupé vied to be the most beautiful car in the world.

The E-Type had one more trump card up its sleeve – it was cheap. Jags had always been good value, and combined with great performance, this had created a slightly unwelcome image. A derogatory term for the middle classes was 'the Jag and gin brigade'. All this was forgotten with the E-Type – it was just too good to knock.

Specifications

Production dates	1961-1973 (all types)
Manufactured units	72,584 (all types)
Engine type	6-cylinder twin overhead cam
Engine size	3,781cc (pre-1964)
Maximum power	265bhp
Transmission	4-speed sychromesh
Top speed	150mph
0-60 mph time	7.1 seconds
Country of origin	UK

'With world-beating performance and looks to die for, it's hard to believe that the E-type was also cheap'

MGB

The MGB was a sports car for every man. The MGB GT was a sports car for every man and his dog

The B was of monocoque construction. This wasn't exactly ground breaking, but the Austin-Healey and Triumph opposition were still built on separate chassis. The mechanical bits came from the rather mundane Austin and Morris saloons. The B series engine was tuned to 95bhp and that meant 100mph. It was enough to make the B an instant bestseller.

In 1965 came a coupé version with small back seats. The clever bit was an opening rear hatch, considerably pre-dating the hatchback boom. The MGB GT's back seats weren't very useful, but there was plenty of room for the dog and the shopping. Practicality meant excellent sales.

There had been interesting variations on the MGB theme. The MGC of 1967 was powered by a modernised version of the 3.0-litre Healey's engine. Unfortunately, it was underpowered, and the weight of the engine ruined the handling. The MGB GT V8 of 1973 was much better. The lightweight Rover V8 meant 125mph and 0 to 60 in just 8 seconds, but only 2,591 of these misunderstood coupés were made.

By the 1970s, the B was long in the tooth, and MG were back to selling simple outdated cars to those who could not embrace modernity. In 1974, the disastrous decision was made to fit all MGBs with the US spec 5mph impact bumpers. The MGB became a bit of a joke – in fact, with hindsight, the rubber bumper cars drive almost identically to earlier cars, but they look awful.

Management indifference and incompetence meant that no successor to the B was developed, and, with complete inevitability, the MG factory closed in 1980.

Specifications

Production dates	1962-1980
Manufactured units	365,000 (MGB); 150,000 (MGB GT)
Engine type	4-cylinder push rod OHV
Engine size	1,798cc
Maximum power	95bhp
Transmission	4-speed sychromesh, optional overdrive, optional automatic – avoid!
Top speed	105mph
0-60 mph time	12.1 seconds
Country of origin	UK

'With excellent
performance and a V8
rumble, the MGB GT
V8 was the best of all
the Bs. It was never
built as a roadster,
and poor management
prevented it from
achieving its potential'

Ford Cortina

Record sales plus record victories made the Mk I 'Tina an all-time classic

There was nothing revolutionary about the car, as all of its mechanical parts came from other Fords, but the sum of its parts was greater, and the crisp-looking 'Tina

was just what the British family man wanted – and at £639, he could afford it.

There soon came a 1500 to add to the 1200, with the option of two or four doors, or an estate. The product planners knew what people wanted, and in 1963 came the GT.

This was the first sporty British Ford, and was the start of a dynasty that continues to this day. With 78bhp, it was capable of reaching 90mph, and with lower suspension and wider wheels it was every boy racer's dream – or it would have been, if the Lotus Cortina

hadn't come along. Colin Chapman's company developed a twin-cam version of Ford's 1500 engine for its Elan, and this was to power the new car. The Lotus cost twice the price of a basic 1200 when new.

In 1966 came the Mk II Cortina, and the final Mk V 'Tina finally bowed out in 1982, being replaced by the Sierra. The Cortina was the UK's best-selling car for two decades.

Specifications

Production dates	1962-1966
Manufactured units	1,013,391
Engine type	4-cylinder, twin cam (Lotus)
Engine size	1,198cc; 1,498cc; 1,558cc (Lotus)
Maximum power	1,200 50bhp; 1,500 61.5bhp; 78bhp (GT); 105bhp (Lotus)
Transmission	4-speed manual with automatic option
Top speed	78mph-107mph
0-60 mph time	8 seconds (Lotus)
Country of origin	UK

JTW 498C

'The Lotus Cortina was a giant killer in its day, its glory on the track reflected in the imagination of every salesman who drove a 1200 Deluxe'

AC Cobra

For some, too much is never enough.
The Cobra is the car for them

After WW2, AC resumed production by putting the

six-cylinder engine they had been making since 1921 into a rather ungainly saloon. Things improved when they adopted a design by John Tojeiro, based rather closely on the contemporary Ferrari Barcetta. This was the AC Ace of 1954, and as well as fitting their own engine, AC also used Bristol and Ford units later on. The Ace, particularly with Bristol power, was quick, good looking, and handled a treat.

In 1961, Bristol stopped making their engine, preferring to utilise the easy power of an American V8, and AC soon followed suit. Texan racing driver Carroll Shelby fitted a Ford V8 to an Ace, and the rest, as they say, is history. Starting with a 4.2-litre, it was soon the 4.7, or 289 cubic inch, that was used.

The 289 was an animal, but the 427 was a monster. To accommodate much fatter rubber, the wheel arches were widened, giving the appearance of a body builder's biceps. No car has ever looked tougher, or had more muscle to back it up. If the 425bhp of the standard 427 wasn't quite enough, you could order up a 485. 'Motor' magazine tested such a car, accelerating to 100mph in a phenomenal 10.1 seconds!

Specifications

Production dates	1962-1969
Manufactured units	560 (289); 510 (427)
Engine type	V8 puhrod OHV
Engine size	4,727cc (289); 6,997cc (427)
Maximum power	270bhp-485bhp
Transmission	4-speed manual
Top speed	160mph
0-60 mph time	4.6 seconds (427)
Country of origin	UK, engine USA

'If imitation really is the sincerest form of flattery, then the Cobra should be the greatest car of all time. Fibreglass kit car replicas have made the shape familiar, but it's still a fabulous-looking car'

Studebaker Avanti

The Avanti was a heroic failure, but one that refused to just lie down and die

In 1938, we saw the first alliance with the creator of the Coke bottle, brilliant industrial designer Raymond Loewy. He was to be involved in all of Studebaker's finest moments.

Loewy Studios styled the whole post-war range. In 1953, Loewy's legendary Starlight coupé was born, which became the Hawk. It was a fabulous car, but circumstances were against it, and 1956 saw the end of the Loewy Studio contract with the company.

By the early 1960s, sales were in the doldrums. Loewy was invited back to create an exotic sports car and revitalise the old company's image, and the result was the Avanti, with styling more innovative than any US car since the Cord. Nothing looked like the Avanti, and although it had never been near a wind tunnel, the sloping

front and high tail meant that it was slippery. It was powered by the Studebaker 289 cubic inch V8. It gave 240bhp, but it was possible to order a supercharger providing 290bhp.

They took a modified car to Bonneville and broke a hatful of records, including running 170.78mph in the flying mile. Unfortunately, problems in making the Avanti's fibreglass body held up its release – deposits were withdrawn and people bought Corvettes. Only a small number were sold before the company moved to Ontario and by 1966 Studebaker was no more.

Specifications

Production dates	1963-1964
Manufactured units	4,643
Engine type	V8, optional supercharger
Engine size	4,733cc
Maximum power	240bhp-290bhp
Transmission	3-speed
Top speed	120mph
0-60 mph time	7.9 seconds
Country of origin	US

'The Avanti's styling was more innovative than any US car since the Cord'

Chevrolet Corvette Stingray

The Stingray was a piece of automotive sculpture – with a V8!

America's first sports car debuted in 1953. It nearly expired in 1955, but then along came the excellent new Small Block V8, and suddenly it was a real sports car.

For 1956 came a smart restyle, and in 1957 a four-speed gearbox and the option of fuel injection. In 1958 there was another restyle, creating more weight, but more power too. In 1961, the rear end got a makeover, giving a subtle hint of what was to come. The fabled Harley Earl had retired as head of GM's Art and Colour section, and Bill Mitchell's era had begun. The 1961 took its back end from a Mitchell styling exercise called the 'Stingray'.

For 1963 there was the first all-new Corvette since 1953 – the Stingray. Mitchell and his team had taken full advantage of the opportunities offered by fibreglass construction to sculpt a truly beautiful body. Design cues were all from the amazing Stingray concept car, while the roadster was now joined by an even more stunning coupé. This dramatic shape had the doors cut into the roof, and the 1963 models had a divided rear screen. These cars are highly sought after.

From the headlights hidden in its pointy nose, to its delicate rear quarter bumpers, it was a hit. Production doubled on the previous year, with around 20,000 cars sold.

Looks were too good to change, and there were only detailed differences year to year. Power went up and up, with a 427 big block for 1966. The ultimate was the L88, with wild 12.5:1 compression ratio and 560bhp, but only 20 were built. Thankfully, disc brakes were now a valuable option.

Specifications

Spec Category	Spec Entry
Production dates	1963 - 1967
Numbers made	117,964
Engine type	V8 pushrod OHV
Engine size	5358 cc/6997 cc
Maximum power	250 bhp to 560 bhp
Transmission	4 speed, optional automatic
Top speed	140 mph - 427
0-60 mph time	4.9 seconds - 427
Country of origin	USA

'So often first is best, and many would say that about the Stingray. The split rear window on the early coupé may have had a cool reception when new but, today, these cars are a collector's dream'

Ford Mustang

Was there ever such a showroom sensation as the '64 Mustang?

The ambitious and able Lee Iacocca had become Ford vice president at the age of 36 in 1960. With the success of the Corvette and imported British sports cars, he saw the opportunity for Ford.

The first result of his

commitment to a new kind of Ford was the Mustang I. It was an impractical, mid-engined concept car, but the public loved it. It didn't take long for the idea to develop into the production Mustang.

Mustang hit the showrooms on April 17th 1964, and it caused a stampede. Demand was beyond the wildest predictions. In fact, demand exceeded supply by 15 to 1. The Mustang became the fastest-selling car in history. Before August 1965, 680,989 had been sold, and the million mark was soon passed.

Ford never called it a 'sports car': the term was 'personal car', and every opportunity was given to buyers to personalise their Mustang.

There was a six and a V8, a hard top and a convertible. These were soon followed by a 2+2 fastback. The options list was huge, and Mustangs could be completely different cars depending on which boxes were ticked at the sale.

The most famous Mustangs were built by Carroll Shelby, creator of the Cobra. His package of modifications brought the 289 up to 306bhp in the Shelby GT-350. Usually white with blue stripes, they became a performance icon.

There were styling changes, but the car remained largely unspoilt until 1969. The new Mustang for 1969 was bigger, heavier and uglier. The glory days were over.

Specifications

Production dates	1964-1969
Manufactured units	2,078,082
Engine type	Straight 6 / V8
Engine size	2,785cc-7,013cc
Maximum power	271bhp (HiPo 289 4735cc)
Transmission	3- or 4-speed manual, optional overdrive / automatic
Top speed	142mph (HiPo 289)
0-60 mph time	6 seconds (HiPo 289)
Country of origin	USA

'Never has a car left the showroom floor as quickly as the '64 Mustang. It was the fastest-selling car in history, and it's not hard to see why'

Pontiac GTO

Big engine, little car. Simple enough, but with the Tempest GTO, the muscle car was born

In the late 1950s, Pontiac had built itself an image based on performance and competition. NASCAR domination worked wonders, but then came the Detroit-wide 'no racing' edict. A new way to preserve the youthful brand image was needed.

Pontiac quite deliberately raised a digit to the whole sports-car world by stealing the name from Ferrari. GTO stood for 'gran turismo omologato', and the 250 GTO was Ferrari's most illustrious sports racer.

In typically American fashion, the Tempest GTO was soon affectionately dubbed the 'Goat'. In a straight line, the $3,800 Goat would outrun the $20,000 Ferrari with ease. Corners would have been a different matter. So would braking, as there wasn't even an option of disc brakes. But at that price, who was complaining?

The GTO Pontiac almost single-handedly invented the muscle car. It was the simple hot-rodding practice of dropping the biggest V8 into the smallest compact sedans and convertibles. The car that would never sell became the company's fastest-selling new model ever.

Acceleration was sensational. With a single carb, the GTO could hit 60 in 6.9 seconds. With the 'Tri-Power' three-carb setup it was 5.7,

hitting 104 in the quarter mile at 14.1 seconds. Nobody much bothered with recording top speeds.

For 1965 there was a restyle, then another for 1966. The 1966 GTO was larger but very good looking, and was now a series all on its own. Jan and Dean sang about it, and its image received another boost when a customised version became the Monkeemobile. The Monkees all got GTOs, and Mike Nesmith was caught speeding on the Hollywood Freeway at 125mph – priceless publicity for Pontiac!

Specifications

Production dates	1964-1967
Manufactured units	286,470
Engine type	V8
Engine size	6,374cc (389 cubic inch)
Maximum power	360bhp
Transmission	3- or 4-speed manual, or 3-speed Hydra-Matic
Top speed	Approx 130mph
0-60 mph time	6.9 seconds
Country of origin	USA

Porsche 911

Few would argue against the 911 being the greatest, and the most enduring, sports car ever

The Porsche 911 is a car that shouldn't work. Hanging the engine out the back might be okay in a 35bhp Beetle, but physics says it isn't going to work in a sports car.

In 1948, Ferdinand Porsche's son,

Ferry, looked to his father's creation, the VW, as the basis for a sports car – the first production Porsche was the 356 of 1950. It started out with a tiny 1,100cc engine, but from the very start the Porsche identity was set.

The 356 got bigger and better engines. Porsche didn't bother with advertising and just went racing instead. The 911 carried on winning like the 356, with dominance in everything from rallying to endurance racing. By now Porsche were building pure racing cars, no longer developed from the road cars, and these were all but unbeatable at Le Mans and in World Sports Car events. The 911 metamorphosed for the track into the

mighty 935, which dominated its class to the point of tedium.

The ultimate early 911 was the 2.7RS of 1972/1973; 210bhp might not sound that impressive, but the RS encapsulated every fine sports-car quality in concentrated form. Fast and raw, with the sharpest steering and perfect balance, the RS has become a Porsche holy grail.

Specifications

Production dates	1964-present
Manufactured units	78,872 to 1973
Engine type	Flat 6, air-cooled, rear-mounted
Engine size	1,991cc; 2,195cc; 2,341cc; 2,687cc
Maximum power	210bhp (2.7RS)
Transmission	5-speed manual or 4-speed Sportmatic
Top speed	153mph (2.7RS)
0-60 mph time	5.5 seconds
Country of origin	Germany

'Engineering and design had overcome physics, and the 911 is held as a paragon of balance and handling'

Alfa Romeo Duetto

*No car has quite embodied 'la dolce vita'
like the little Alfa Spider*

The first mass-produced Alfa was the 1900 of 1950. It was a rather dull-looking saloon. In 1955 it was replaced by the smaller, sharper Giulietta, a range of cars of which each model was to be based on the same mechanicals. These cars were very advanced for 1955, with twin overhead cam all-alloy engines, five-speed gearboxes and clever, lightweight monocoque bodies. The engines, in modified form,were to last over 40 years.

First to surface was the Giulietta Sprint. It was an achingly pretty coupé designed by Bertone, and it could crack 100mph. There was also a saloon, and in the summer of 1955 came the Giulietta Spider. The open car had a different look to the coupé because it was designed by another of Italy's great studios: Pininfarina. It was a very sophisticated little car, and Alfa Romeo sold all that it could make. In 1962 it got a 1,570cc engine and became the Giulia Spider.

For 1966 the Giulia Spider was given a completely new look. At the time, the jury was out on the new styling, some thinking it lacked the finesse of the old shape, some saying it wasn't modern enough. As the most popular and enduring of all Alfas, it now seems hard to believe.

Released without a name, a competition was held and 'Duetto' was the winner. Unfortunately it was also the name of a well-known snack, so it only lasted a year. With a sharply cut-off tail that arrived in 1967, the Spider carried on well into the 1980s.

Specifications

Production dates	1966-1967
Manufactured units	6,325
Engine type	4-cylinder twin overhead cams
Engine size	1,570cc
Maximum power	109bhp
Transmission	5-speed synchromesh
Top speed	111mph
0-60 mph time	11.3 seconds
Country of origin	Italy

'The Duetto will forever be associated with the carefree 1960s, as lovestruck Dustin Hoffman's car in "The Graduate"'

Lamborghini Miura

Ferruccio's Miura set the standard for supercars, and remains the most beautiful in perpetuity

In 1961 there was something of a walkout at Ferrari. Enzo was infamous for his conservatism. Frustration at their inability to realize their ideas led to the departure of six of their

top designers and engineers. One was Ferruccio Lamborghini. Producing tractors and air-conditioning systems had made him wealthy, and now he decided to beat Enzo at his own game. Giotto Bizzarrini, who had designed the immortal Ferrari 250 GTO, designed a fabulous new engine for Lamborghini. It was technically what Bizzarrini had wanted the GTO to be, but the styling was a little dubious and sales were disappointing. A similar 400GT followed, but it was in 1966 that Ferruccio staked a genuine claim on immortality.

His engineers still wanted to go racing. The mid-engined layout was now ubiquitous on the track, but the length of the V12 engine was a problem. Dallara

and the other Ferrari renegades came up with the brilliant idea of placing the engine transversely, across the car behind the driver. The Miura P400 took the 1966 Geneva Motor Show by storm. It was a technical marvel, with the engine block, gearbox, and final drive all made in one complex casting. It performed as good as it looked, completely rewriting the sports-car rules.

There followed a more powerful S model, and the ultimate SV in 1971, capable of over 170mph. In 1974 the Countach took over. It was shocking and sensational, but it wasn't beautiful.

Specifications

Production dates	1966-1972
Manufactured units	765
Engine type	V12 4-cam, transverse rear-mounted
Engine size	3,929cc
Maximum power	350bhp (SV 385bhp)
Transmission	5-speed in unit with engine
Top speed	171mph
0-60 mph time	5.5 seconds
Country of origin	Italy

Dodge Charger

*The muscle car's flowering was short but vibrant;
the R/T Hemi Charger was brightest of them all*

In 1966 the Dodge Charger was born. It was built, 'to bite deep into the Pontiac GTO belt'. The

Charger was based on the mid-sized Coronet, but with a distinctive fastback roof line and hidden headlights. The standard engine was the 318 cubic inch V8, bolted into the Charger it would get you to 60mph in 5.3 seconds. In 1968 the second-generation Charger was created – a shape known to those who watched 'The Dukes of Hazzard'. More memorably, it was the bad guys' car in the greatest car chase ever filmed, seen pursued by Steve McQueen's Boss Mustang in 'Bullitt'. The sleek new shape could now be seen wearing an R/T badge if

a 440 or a 426 cubic inch engine was lurking under the hood. The Hemi was still too rich for most – only 475 '68s got sold.

The Charger didn't do as well in NASCAR as had been hoped, so for 1969 a homologation special was made with an outrageous aerodynamic package. A wing towered feet above the trunk and the nose was long and tapering. Less obviously the rear window was different, to make it work better at the 200mph that stock cars were now reaching.

Specifications

Production dates	1966-1970
Manufactured units	238,936
Engine type	V8
Engine size	6,980cc (Hemi); 7,210cc (440 Magnum)
Maximum power	425bhp (Hemi); 375bhp (440 Magnum)
Transmission	4-speed or Torqueflite automatic
Top speed	Approx 140mph
0-60 mph time	5.3 seconds
Country of origin	USA

'...*for 1969 a homologation special was made with an outrageous aerodynamic package. A wing towered feet above the trunk and the nose was long and tapering...*'

Scimitar GTE

The world's first high-speed estate makes the perfect classic... but nobody's noticed

The reliant Scimitar GTE was innovative, had high profile royal patronage, and it makes a fast, stylish, and remarkably practical classic.

Reliant made three-wheelers. The nasty three-wheelers were constructed from fibreglass and, due to their expertise with the new material, Reliant helped develop a car for the Israelis. The first car was a version of this called the Sabre. Although horrid and slow, with a restyle and a six-cylinder Ford engine, it was better, even if rather old-fashioned, cramped, and expensive.

Sales were hampered by the lack of proper rear seats, and Ogle were asked to come up with an answer. There had been a Triplex Glass show car with a glass estate rear grafted onto the coupé. This proved the inspiration for a whole new kind of car.

In 1968 the GTE was unveiled. It shared its running gear with the Coupé, but the chassis was new, as was the fibreglass body. The styling, however, was still plainly related. There were four proper seats and a glass hatchback, and yet it was still most certainly a sports car – and an elegant one at that.

Princess Anne was a loyal and vocal supporter of the marque, owning several examples. The GTE sold well, and with 1975 came a redesign. Although a bigger, less attractive car, it still sold. Unfortunately there was never the investment to develop a successor and in 1986 the GTE died.

Specifications

Production dates	1968-1986
Manufactured units	14,273
Engine type	V6
Engine size	2,994cc
Maximum power	138bhp
Transmission	4-speed optional overdrive; automatic
Top speed	121mph
0-60 mph time	9.3 seconds
Country of origin	UK

Datsun 240Z

As the British dropped the sports car baton, the Japanese picked it up, and the 240Z became the best-selling sports car of all time

The Japanese were still happy to copy the best, and the engine they had put together for their saloons was uncannily similar to Mercedes' six-cylinder unit. With suitable running gear from the

Bluebird, they were now in search of a body. It was to be no larger than a Porsche 911, and concern over increasingly paranoid US safety legislation meant that an open car was ruled out.

There is much discussion over who actually styled the car. The Austrian count, Albrecht Goertz, certainly had a lot to do with it. The car took its cues from all the best sources: there was a good deal of E-Type, some 911, and maybe some Aston in there. The resulting

240Z was unoriginal, but very pleasing.

The engineering was equally conventional, but again, it came from the best sources. Many compared the driving experience to the Austin Healey 3000.

The 240Z not only took over from where the Healey stopped – it took over and took off. The Americans loved it so much that the 240Z and its successors became the best-selling sports cars in history. In 1973, the 240Z was replaced by the 260Z, but from there on the Z cars got bigger and softer.

Specifications

Production dates	1969-1973
Manufactured units	172,767
Engine type	Straight 6
Engine size	2,393cc
Maximum power	151bhp
Transmission	4-speed or automatic (USA); 5-speed only (Europe)
Top speed	125mph
0-60 mph time	8.0 seconds
Country of origin	Japan

BMW 3.0 CSL

A fabulous road car, the 'Batmobile' was to make the European Touring Car Championship its own

Although having been around since 1916, BMW's first car of 1928 was the Dixi. The manufacturer's engineering advanced rapidly, and by the late 1930s it was building some very

advanced cars. It was the 'Neue Klasse' 1500 of 1961 that was to set the future direction for the company. There was a single overhead camshaft engine and independent suspension all round. It was a sharply styled, thoroughly modern car, and it sold. In 1966 came the 1602, soon joined by the 2002 – the small saloons that were to establish BMW as a volume manufacturer.

A 2.0-litre coupé appeared in 1966; initially odd-looking, it became a beauty in 1968 with a new nose and a six-cylinder engine. In 1971, the 2800CS became the 3.0CS, with fuel injection available on the CSi, offering 200bhp and 130mph. car. In 1972, BMW built the CSL, a homologation

special, to give the racers the parts they needed. These included alloy body panels, minimal trim, and a reduction in weight. Engines were 3,003cc, and later 3,153cc. Most striking were the aerodynamic modifications. But what everybody remembers is the rear wing. This device provided enough downforce to stop the cars getting loose at the back at high speed. It also gave it the nickname of 'The Batmobile'.

Specifications

Production dates	1972-1975
Manufactured units	1,039
Engine type	Straight 6-single overhead cam
Engine size	3,303; 3,153cc
Maximum power	206bhp (400+ for racing)
Transmission	4-speed
Top speed	137mph
0-60 mph time	7.4 seconds
Country of origin	Germany

'The BMW 3.0 CSL road car – the everyday version of the 'Batmobile' thattook Touring Cars Racing by storm'

'The Duesenberg SJ – one of the
finest classic cars to grace the earth...'